MY KID
ON
DRUGS?
NEVER!

BEN WICKS

Published in 1993 by
Alliance for a Drug-Free Canada
PO Box 355 Station A Toronto, Ontario M5W 1C5
In co-operation with
Addiction Research Foundation
33 Russell Street, Toronto, Ontario M5S 2S1
ISBN 0-88868-203-4

This book is dedicated to Mark Nussbaum, a friend who suggested that I reach out to those parents in need of help

CONTENTS

INTRODUCTION

It seemed like only yesterday your kids were attempting to crawl across the room. Now all too quickly they are venturing out into the world.

They no longer seem to need us. The telephone never stops ringing and it's always for them. New faces appear at the door as their circle of friends begins to expand. We have suddenly become "just parents."

We are no longer the decision makers. Now the kids are ready to ask their own questions and make decisions of their own.

They are convinced that they are better than we are at thinking things through and they are determined to stand on their own feet.

By the ages of ten to 15 they are prepared to explore and share the world outside with others, but they face a world that is far different from the one in which we grew up.

You may think you had it tough, but try to put yourself in their position. They are bombarded with the news that the ozone layer is thinning, the rain forests are being destroyed, the air we breathe is polluted, that rivers and streams are dying and even the ocean itself is to be avoided.

DON'T SPEAK TO STRANGERS, STAY OUT OF THE SUN AND DON'T GO NEAR ANY WATER

Via television, today's youth witnesses horrors wherever they occur: natural disasters, starvation in the developing world or a killing in the next block.

It's enough to make most people reach out for something to ease the pain of a world gone mad.

AND NOW, IF I MAY, A SPECIAL PRAYER FOR THOSE PARENTS WITH TEEN AGERS

Despite this, the majority of today's youth scramble over the mess in which we have left the world and are ready to make their way successfully to maturity.

Many of them have experimented with some form of drug, usually tobacco and alcohol, for a variety of reasons. Happily most of them have not become dependent.

Does this mean that drugs are not a problem? Of course drugs are a problem. Does this mean I support the taking of drugs? Nothing could be further from the truth.

Finding that your child is using drugs can be a shock. Reacting to the news in a way that drives the child to continue using the substance can lead to disaster.

Hopefully this book will assist you should you be faced with a child who has a problem of excessive drug use. The cartoons throughout are intended to lighten the message without detracting from the seriousness of the subject.

This book should be used as a guide and is not intended to replace professional treatment, should it be necessary.

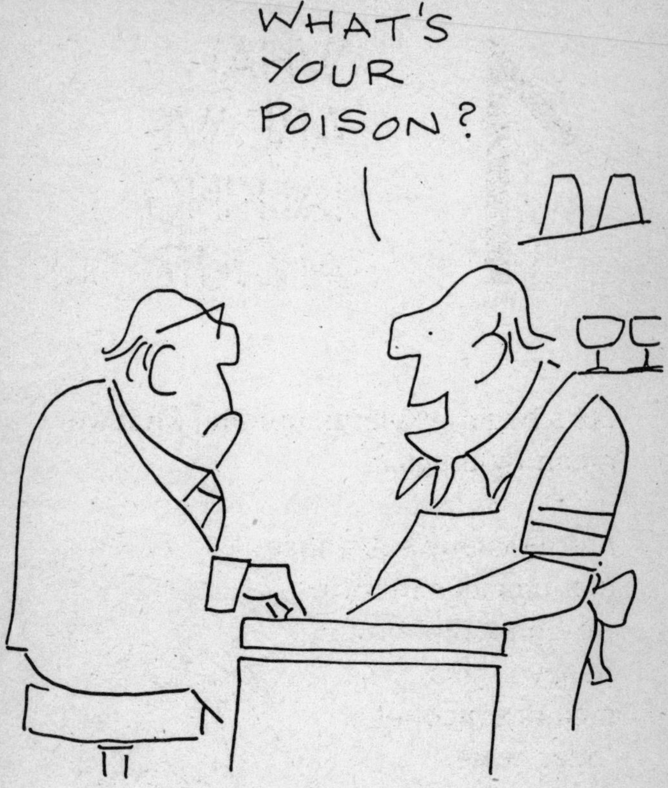
WHAT'S YOUR POISON?

1 WHAT ARE WE TALKING ABOUT?

Let's begin by understanding what we mean by drugs.

A drug is any substance that changes the way we think, feel or behave. This includes alcohol (beer, wine, liquor), tobacco, caffeine (coffee, tea, cola), prescription drugs and chemicals in various consumer products that can be sniffed.

All of these drugs can be harmful if used in such a way as to affect our health and social welfare.

Any drug, even those drugs that we think of as safe, can be dangerous. The risk is in the amount that is taken or the length of time over which the drug is used.

"You mean if I have a headache I should just

TAKE ONE AFTER MEALS

hold my head and hope for the best?" Not at all. The advances that have been made in medicine are astounding.

Many ailments, once painful or life threatening, can now be cured. Taking something for a headache once in a while is a long way from frantically popping tranquillizers and sleeping pills.

What we are concerned with here are those drugs that can become addictive or create dependency — alcohol, street drugs and drugs meant to relieve pain, calm nerves or induce sleep.

So let's take a closer look at the drugs that head the list of any parent's concerns.

2 DRUGS? WHAT DRUGS?

We hear about drugs every day — crack, ecstasy, ice, dope — yet how many of us know what they really are? All we do know about the subject is that "It's something that my kids shouldn't do."

HIC!

As parents we all want to keep our children safe, and to do that, we need to know what they risk if they use drugs. That way we talk with them honestly about drugs.

Let's start with alcohol and tobacco. They are the two most common drugs and those that the average kid is likely to experience first.

LET'S SAY I HAVE SIX GIN AND TONICS — IF I DRINK TWO, HOW MANY HAVE I GOT LEFT?

TOBACCO
- Tobacco is the largest preventable cause of premature death in the developed world.

This fact should certainly scare your kids away from tobacco, right? Wrong!

The last thing that kids are worried about is something that is going to affect their health a million years down the road.

Sure they've seen some poor devil dying of emphysema on television saying he wished he'd quit smoking, but young smokers are convinced it will never happen to them.

ALCOHOL
- Like tobacco, use of this drug in our society is common.

Unfortunately, like tobacco, there are long-term health risks associated with alcohol use: destruction of the liver, cancer and brain damage, to name a few.

But there are other risks to be considered.

Thousands of young people have been killed and continue to die on our highways in automobile accidents that involve alcohol.

Remember, although alcohol and tobacco are legal for use by adults, this does not include under-age youth.

MARIJUANA

- Marijuana is also known as dope, pot and weed, and is usually the first street drug tried by kids. It looks like ground-up, dried leaves.

- It is usually smoked, although it can be added to baked goods and eaten. Rolled into a cigarette shape and lit, it gives off smoke that is high in tar, and tar causes lung cancer.

JIMMY SAID HIS FIRST WORD TODAY— MARIJUANA

- Long time users of marijuana often lack motivation. When high, users may be clumsy and uncoordinated and appear drunk. Naturally this heightens the risk of traffic and other accidents.
- Since marijuana is a street drug, users can never be sure of what they're getting. They may be paying for marijuana that is contaminated with weed killers or other toxic substances.

And that's not all. Depending on where your child is getting the drug, he may be associating with people who pose a risk to him in a variety of ways.

STIMULANTS
- Stimulants do just what the name suggests — they stimulate us.

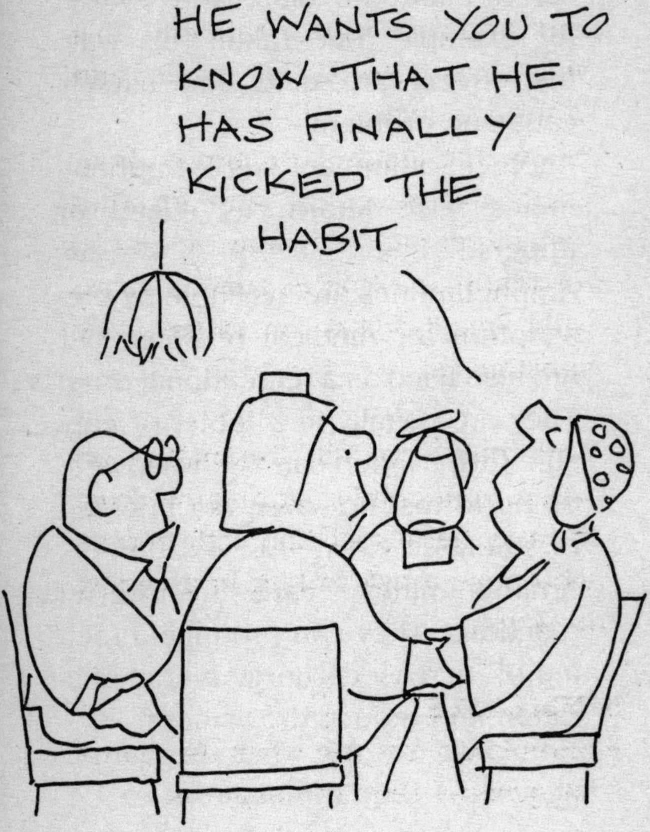
HE WANTS YOU TO KNOW THAT HE HAS FINALLY KICKED THE HABIT

Our kids are often exposed to caffeine before any other drug — in soft drinks, chocolate and coffee, for example. But, taken this way, the effects are mild and usually cause no problems.

- Another stimulant is amphetamines, also known as speed or uppers.
- Amphetamines are available by prescription for medical reasons, but are also used as a recreational drug.
- They are usually in a tablet or capsule form, which can be swallowed. Some forms, however, are injected or smoked.
- Amphetamines cause powerful reactions. They can produce a feeling of increased energy and exhilaration and reduce drowsiness.

- Side effects of amphetamine use include insomnia, agitation and loss of appetite. Long-time users may develop psychoses, experience hallucinations or behave violently.

COCAINE
- Cocaine is probably the most talked-about stimulant, along with the form of cocaine called "crack."
- It is extracted from the leaves of the coca plant.
- Cocaine is a white, odorless powder, which can be rubbed into the gums or "snorted" up the nose.

- A "line" or "hit" of cocaine is a ridge of powder about two to five inches long by one-quarter inch wide. It is snorted through a straw or rolled-up paper money, or from a long fingernail or coke spoon (often worn around the neck).
- Cocaine can also be dissolved in water and injected in a vein.
- Cocaine causes feelings similar to those produced by amphetamines — a sense of power and energy and the delusion that one can do anything.
- Long-term use can lead to dependence, where the user craves the drug.

- Your child may begin using cocaine by snorting it or rubbing it on his or her gums, but the even greater risk is that he may eventually start to inject it.
- The use of cocaine, or any drug, by intravenous injection is incredibly risky behaviour. Needle use can expose the user to hepatitis or HIV (the virus that causes AIDS). **Using drugs intravenously can kill.**

CRACK
- It's still cocaine, but its form has been altered slightly so that it can be smoked.
- Crack is made by dissolving cocaine in water and adding baking soda or other chemicals. This results in a hard paste that, once dried, can be broken into small pieces.

- The term *crack* may come from the sound that the pieces make when they are burned.
- Crack can be smoked in a cigarette, from a pop can or through a water pipe.
- Because crack reaches the brain quickly when smoked, it produces effects similar to those of injected cocaine. A real risk is that the next step could be injecting cocaine.

There are many other drugs, of course. Heroin causes relief from pain and dulls one's emotions. It is usually injected into a vein, but other similar drugs, like codeine, can be ingested by mouth.

Inhalants are chemicals, such as gasoline or glue fumes, which are inhaled, often from a plastic bag.

Other types of drugs are hallucino-
gens, such as LSD, sedatives, like bar-
biturates, and tranquillizers, such as
Valium.

Drug use is often a progression, from
cigarettes and alcohol to marijuana to
other drugs, perhaps injected.

The kid who doesn't smoke tobacco
cigarettes is less likely to try marijuana than the kid who does.

The kid who smokes crack is more
likely to start injection drug use than
the kid who you caught sneaking a
bottle of beer.

Do you, as a parent, have a potential
problem? Let's start by asking the
question, "Why do kids take drugs?"

3 WHY DO KIDS TAKE DRUGS?

We live in a chemical world. Wherever we turn, the message bombards us: drugs solve our problems. Can't sleep? Take a pill. Have a headache? Get rid of it with two of these. Want to lose weight? This will do the trick.

OKAY— I'VE TAKEN A PILL— NOW WHO'S THE FAIREST IN THE LAND?

Whatever we want to do is simple. Just take drugs.

Is it any wonder that young people develop a curiosity about drugs? (The real mystery may be why more children don't follow in the footsteps of addicted parents, friends and heroes.)

So why do kids take drugs? Many experiment with drugs because they are bored. Some are curious. With all the talk about drugs, they are tempted to find out what they are like.

They feel rebellious. They believe they have reached an age when they must declare their independence. Some seek an escape. What better way to avoid a problem than by numbing the mind to whatever is happening at school or in the home?

But the most common reason for taking drugs is primarily that they want to be like their friends. The motivation is from *within*.

Your child may want to be part of the "cool" group. It's certainly a lot easier to do what the
other kids are
doing
than to
walk
away.

It's easy to forget that we were once adolescents, trying to find our way in the world. Some changes are simply part of growing up.

Certainly our children are struggling to spread their wings. Whether in a school playground or in a park, they no longer have an adult watching their every move.

Their world is more confusing and complex than the one we experienced as adolescents.

Adolescence is probably one of the most stressful times in our lives. Remember when you were a teenager and had to deal with all those "impossible" problems?

"I'll never pass the exam tomorrow!" "My folks just don't understand!" "There's a huge zit on my nose just a day before my big date!"

"If I don't go along with this I'll lose all my friends."

"Do teachers think that homework is all there is to life?"

How do you handle all this without having established coping skills? It's not easy, and some of us don't help matters by telling our teens that, "If you think things are tough now wait 'till you become an adult." Great! You mean it gets worse than this?

As our children struggle to sort out their lives, some decide that certain substances might make the world less threatening. Maybe they're sharing a cigarette behind the school or "borrowing" a beer from the fridge. We know what that was like; we did it too. But there's a difference between a casual puff and a situation that calls for your intervention.

4 IS THERE A PROBLEM?

Are we dealing with a hidden enemy or are kids just being kids? Are drugs really a problem for my child?

Any regular use of a substance with a desirable effect may result in negative effect or a set behaviour pattern. You may never actually see the chemicals being used, but the changes in behaviour will usually be clear.

Here are some of the signs you should look for that indicate there is reason to be concerned about your kids:

* They are continually depressed or undergo a sudden change in behaviour and appearance that can't be accounted for.
* Their attitude towards you or other family members is not what it was.
* They spend most of their time in their rooms.
* They avoid family meals.
* Kids who were once helpful around the house are no longer willing to lend a hand.
* Their school grades drop.
* Your kids have new friends whom they rarely, if ever, bring to the house. (The new friends may be older, troubled youths who are themselves drug users.)

* Your children have wild mood swings.
* They suffer from recurring respiratory ailments.
* They show signs of intoxication (bloodshot eyes, slurred speech and/or lack of coordination).
* They are preoccupied with money, constantly borrowing from members of the family.
* Money is missing from around the house.
* Drug paraphernalia (pipes, rolling papers, eye droppers, camera-film containers and plastic bags) is in evidence.

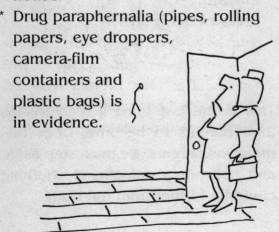

A new world is opening up to your children, as cool friends appear who can be counted on to sympathize when "boring and out of touch parents" who "don't understand" dispense advice or direction.

Unfortunately many parents attempt to become "more hip" often to the chagrin of their teens.

This is the last thing a teen wishes their parents to become. Does this mean, as parents, we must step aside and become onlookers? Nothing could be further from the truth.

What the teens seek more than anything else is understanding. Just ask yourself these two important questions:

WHAT IS THE RISK TO MY KID? HOW DO WE WORK TOGETHER TO GET RID OF THAT RISKY BEHAVIOUR?

IF YOU DON'T WANT TO GET HIGH, WHAT DO YOU WANT TO DO?

5 WHAT CAN I DO?

Don't panic. Suppose you feel that your child is exhibiting one or more of the above symptoms.

Approach the problem as you would any other you may have faced with your child in the past . It's true that this is not a "wash-behind-your-ears" situation.

Remember, what you have observed may be totally unrelated to drugs and merely a natural stage in the process of growing up.

Don't jump to conclusions, but don't ignore the evidence and tell yourself that things will turn out just fine.

Draw up a check-list of behaviour changes. If your child has always found school difficult, then a failed grade is obviously not a change of pattern. If, on the other hand, your child was an A student who suddenly has a C— average, it's cause for concern.

Although we have mentioned it in chapter two, let us look again at one of the most common causes of behaviour changes in children — alcohol.

Drinking in our society is so common that it's easy to ignore the fact that there is danger in taking a drink.

Expectant mothers face the added danger of fetal alcohol syndrome. A drinking habit can directly affect the unborn child. This is directly related to unsafe levels of alcohol consumption during pregnancy. It is totally avoidable! Prevention starts as early as prenatally.

Hic!

Alcohol is a drug and must be seen as such.
The child who is drinking is on a drug. Alcohol, no matter what form it's in — beer, wine or liquor — is still a drug.

Let's look at three drinks and see what they contain. A bottle of beer has the same effect as 5 ounces of wine or 1 1/2 ounces of liquor.

Children get hooked on alcohol much faster than adults do.

It's also a fact that the earlier children start drinking regularly, the more likely they are to have a problem with alcohol later in life.

As well, the earlier children use alcohol the more prone they are to move onto other drugs.

Kids who abuse alcohol will find that they are missing out on many of the pleasures of their youth. Relaxing will be difficult for them and finding ways to have fun will not be easy without the drug.

Accidents will be common. Whether it be a car, snowmobile or powerboat, the risk of an alcohol-related accident is always there. Even the riding of a bike or losing their balance when walking or running can place the drinker in dangerous situations.

The loss of their inhibitions might cause them to say or do things that they will regret later. Their behaviour will not be conducive to making friends.

We know that peer influence can steer a child into negative actions, but it can work in some kids' favour too. Friends committed to a healthy lifestyle can also affect one's choices.

Speaking of friends, you can help your child to find friends. Notice that I said find them, not choose them.

FRANKIE MEET JANE

Encourage them to join some of the many groups that are available. Try the Boy Scouts, Girl Guides, YM/ YWCA, recreation centres, sports teams or library programs, for starters.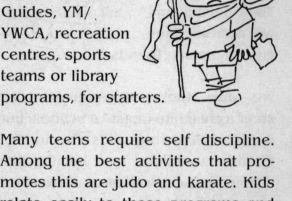

Many teens require self discipline. Among the best activities that promotes this are judo and karate. Kids relate easily to these programs and more effort should be made to encourage their involvement in them.

Bringing up kids in this world is tough. Many parents, for whatever reason, find themselves facing the task alone. Whether single or as a couple, today's parents are faced with hurdles over which they must help their children.

To discover that their child is hooked on drugs is a parents' nightmare. They quickly find themselves running through the gamut of emotions — denial, anger, blame, remorse, etc.

It's a natural reaction and one that most parents respond to in the same way.

* A feeling of a violation of trust and confidence.
* A potential exists for influencing younger brothers and siblings.
* The stupidity of the act.
* Their inability to deal with their children's rationalizations i.e., "I'm not hurting anyone but myself."

Others may turn a blind eye to the danger and feel convinced that this is something that happens only to other people's children.

All too often parents have noticed a worrisome aspect of  their child's behaviour but have satisfied themselves that the child is just going through a phase. He or she will get over it.

When this doesn't happen and parents have faced the fact that their child is abusing some substance, what can they do about it?

Kick in the door of the child's room? Go down on bended knee? Maybe bribing is the answer.

Is there something wrong with you as a parent?  Maybe you were too soft on your child. Maybe you were too tough. It's enough to make you crazy. You just don't know what to do.

Have you considered more structure for your child? Most homes have certain rules of behaviour. "From six to eight it's homework time," or "Yes, you can go out, but you must be home by . . . " and so on. Rules may also include your child taking out the garbage or walking the dog. If there are no rules in your house, it may be a good idea to lay some down.

Everyone in the house has to agree to abide by them. It must be understood by all that breaking these rules will result in certain privileges being revoked from whomever broke the rule.

Remember this is a *family* agreement. That means the adults in the house must obey them too.

For example, if the kids are bothered by their parents' smoke, they have a right to ask that a non- smoking rule be established.

GO TO YOUR ROOM

If your kids do something that you're not happy with, tell them what was wrong with what they did, not what's wrong with *them*.

The key is being close enough for them to know that you are there when needed and ready to support them. Be there to remind them that you understand.

If, like the rest of us, you sometimes say things to them that you later regret, *tell* them you're sorry.

ER -

If they did a good job let them know about it. *Tell* them that you're proud of them and that their room looks great now that their clothes are off the floor.

Most important of all, let them know that you love them. Show it — give them a hug.

6 ARE YOU PART OF THE PROBLEM?

Are you doing everything you can to help your child lead a healthy life?

Do you smoke? Do you drink?

Sure, you may do both. It's your right. But it strains credibility to lecture your kids about the dangers of smoking with a cigarette dangling from your mouth or to need a drink to recover from your talk about the dangers of drug abuse.

What can you do?
Plenty. Start by
setting a good
example.

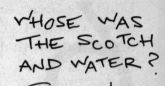

Watching you
drink can
encourage a
child to try
alcohol. If
you are

having a group of friends over to the
house, explain to your child that
drinking is not the reason for getting
together.

And, please, don't encourage your
children to help you mix or serve
drinks. Unfortunately, many kids will
know how to do this soon enough.
They don't need you to point the way.

Don't let them take sips from your glass. Children are naturally curious about a drink that you may be holding. That is no excuse for you to amuse yourself at their expense. Remember that a taste can lead to a sip and a sip to a drink.

So you smoke. You should know that tobacco is a drug, a drug that kills more people than all other drugs combined.

Smoking can cause heart disease, cancer and serious breathing problems. Tell your child that it's an addictive drug and, once people are hooked, it is extremely difficult to stop.

Since most children are not impressed by the fact that smoking two packs a day for 30 years can cut your life span by eight years (30 years is a lifetime when you're 12), you'll need a new approach.

Explain that smoking makes your breath, clothes and hair smell bad.

Explain that smoking will affect your child's ability to play sports as the damaged lungs of a smoker have to work much harder to compete with the non-smokers in the school.

Last, and by no means least, remind them that smoking is expensive. Spending money on cigarettes will mean that there is less for other forms of entertainment.

Why am I being so tough on tobacco? For the simple fact that children who start to smoke are more likely to try other drugs.

Even if you smoke, you can make your children aware of the dangers.

Try to limit your smoking. Try not to smoke in the house, and certainly never smoke in the close confines of a car, especially when children are travelling with you.

Although the solutions for a potential drug problem appear simple, we all know it is difficult. But remember, we're speaking about the health of your children. What could be more important?

Maybe it's time you re-examined your drug taking behavior. How many aspirin are you taking a day? And what about those wonderful slimming pills?

And don't forget the cough medicine that is always on hand. Few of us can deny that we are guilty at some time in our child's life of persuading them to take some form of prescription drug. This is natural.

But how often do we give our children a healthy dose of self-worth? It's as vital as any medicinal pick-me-up.

Too many parents feel that poking fun at their children is just that — having fun. All too often the element of fun is a weapon that destroys self-esteem as effectively as any biting comment.

HEY FATTY — HOW WAS SCHOOL TODAY?

The fact is that the issue of self-worth is critical and must be fed and nurtured. It is the critical issue in any discussion involving teens, kids and drugs. More than that. It is the one thing that all drug users have in common. A feeling of non-worth.

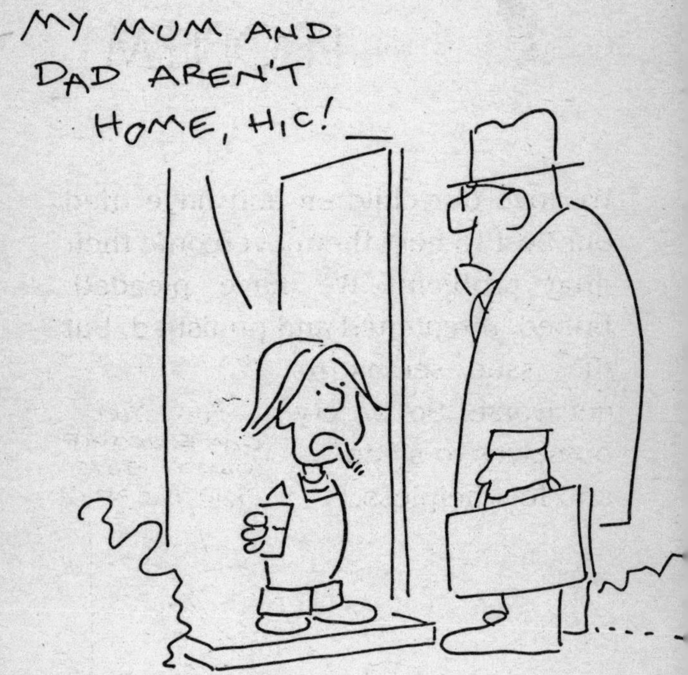
MY MUM AND DAD AREN'T HOME, HIC!

7 I REALLY DO HAVE A PROBLEM

We love our children and have tried our best to help them overcome their drug problem. We have pleaded, bribed, threatened and punished, but the issue seems to get worse. So we cry ourselves to sleep and feel helpless.

Experience has shown that those needing help are often the last to realize there is a problem.

They continue to deny that they are addicted, even though they see their world collapsing around them. **This denial is a crucial sign of being addicted**.

All too often it takes a drastic occurrence to finally persuade the addict that something must be done.

Trouble with the law, the threat of being thrown out of school or the danger of losing a job can force your child to finally seek treatment.

But it is not easy persuading addicts that they have a problem and that it is affecting those closest to them.

Before seeking expert help, have you explored the use of others who love and care for the one with the problem?

Someone whom the teen or child respects and admires. One whose thoughts and opinions matter.

Maybe it's one of these:

Brother/Sister.
Girlfriend/Boyfriend.
Adult role model.
And believe it or not — grandparents.

Most kids have good relations with their grandparents. In many cases better than with the parents.

Despite everything we've discussed it's time for me to repeat something I mentioned earlier.

DO *NOT* PANIC.

Two-thirds of kids grow out of the need for drugs and lead healthy and responsible lives.

Despite this reassurance you do feel that you have a problem.

You have tried and found that the the time for expert help has arrived.

There are no half measures. The only answer to your kid's problem is to stop drug use.

The family should be aware that each and every member will be a vital link in any treatment process.

Family members, more than anyone, know the disruption caused by advanced stages of drug addiction. Already hurt, they may find that the early stages of treatment can be an equally difficult time for both their child and themselves.

For this reason it is essential that detoxification (the process of getting drugs out of the body) be done under medical supervision.

Before this can begin, a professional counselor will need to know the kind of drug taken and the way it has been used. This information will help the staff to decide on the most appropriate treatment.

Fortunately there are now a large number of treatment centres with various drug treatment programs available.

Although the problem appears to demand expert medical attention what is usually overlooked is the role that can be played by the school.

Working in conjunction with the clinic the school can prove to be a major player. Many surveys have shown that those outpatient clinics working with the schools have had a greater degree of success than those working independently.

The hurt, pain and shame experienced by the addict and all members of the family can only be arrested by total abstinence.

The first moments of recovery can be difficult and extremely delicate. It will help to understand what is involved in the treatment process.

OUTPATIENT CLINICS

These allow people to attend school or work while they receive treatment. Some clinics require the individual to attend several evenings a week; others require only a few hours a week.

INPATIENT FACILITIES

Treatment usually lasts from three to five weeks and is offered by hospitals or public treatment centres. Only those facilities that insist on after-care should be considered.

RESIDENTIAL PROGRAMS

These programs may last from several months to a year and are for those with extremely serious problems. They were originally started for heroin addicts but now include severe cocaine or alcohol abusers.

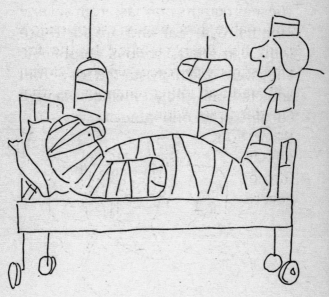

8 WHAT IS THE TREATMENT LIKE?

The battle has begun. Your child's body has been changed by the foreign substance forced upon it. Now it will undergo other changes as that substance is withdrawn. The effects may be severe.

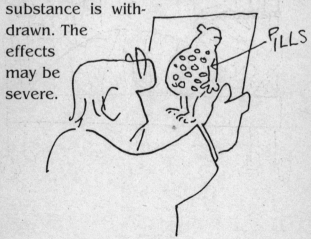

PILLS

Once the treatment is over, the after-care program begins. This stage is critical to a successful recovery, as it lasts a lifetime.

It is often said that true recovery begins the first day after treatment.

SEE YOU NEXT WEEK

Regular visits to the the treatment centre must be maintained.

Depending on the particular drug problem, patients are often introduced to self-help groups such as Alcoholics Anonymous (AA), Narcotics Anonymous (NA) or Cocaine Anonymous (CA).

If you need more information, your local hospital, treatment or assessment centre will be more than pleased to help.

WHAT THE HELL'S GOING ON?

DON'T ASK ME—I'M A FOREIGNER IN THESE PARTS

9 CONCLUSION

Concern for your children is not enough. You'll need to show that you love them.

Communicate with them. When they come home from school, ask them about the kind of day they had. And most important of all, **listen to what they say**.

SO HOW WAS YOUR DAY?

It sounds silly, but learning to listen in a world of noise can be one of the most difficult skills to develop. The television is on.

The radio is playing. You're in the middle of a good book, and the newspaper has just arrived.

Give your kids a break. What they have to say is more important than all the daytime soap operas put together.

Turn off the TV and radio *and listen*. The book and newspaper will still be there when the kids are in bed.

It is not easy to be a good listener.

COME QUICK, KIDS—
DADDY'S MAKING
A PERSONAL
APPEARANCE

It takes work, but I promise you the effort is worth it. Maybe the news your kid is bringing will not affect the way the world turns. It may not interest you but to your child it could be vital.

So *listen* when they tell you that a friend no longer likes them. *Listen* when they tell you about a new teacher. Let them know that you feel for them.

If it's good news, be happy with them. If it's sad, sympathize. And if it's a problem, let them know that you are prepared to help them solve it.

Don't interrupt. Let them take their time and tell you in their own words. Repeat back to them what they have said. This way they will know that you have heard and you understand.

There will be times when it is impossible for you to give them your full attention right when they want it.

Explain why you cannot give them that attention and promise to listen to their news later. **And don't forget. Keep that promise**.

After all, kids are like us. They have their off days, their lousy days when nothing seems to go right. They can be just as tired, just as crabby and just as moody as we sometimes are.

The good news is that they can be just as much fun, just as happy, just as thoughtful, just as kind and, well, just as human as we are.

Information Resources

Canadian Centre on Substance Abuse/National Clearinghouse
on Substance Abuse
112 Kent Street, Suite 480
Ottawa, Ontario
K1P 5P2 (613) 235-4048

PROVINCIAL

BRITISH COLUMBIA

Alcohol & Drug Programmes
1019 Wharf Street, 3rd floor
Victoria, BC   V8V 1X4

BC Prevention Resource
  Centre
96 East Broadway, Suite 108
Vancouver, BC   V5T 1V6
(604) 874-8452

ALBERTA

AADAC/Alberta Alcohol &
  Drug Abuse Commission
10909 Jasper Avenue,
  2nd floor
Edmonton, Alberta   T5J 3M9
(403) 427-2837
Library: (403) 427-7303

SASKATCHEWAN

SADAC/Saskatchewan Alcohol
  & Drug Abuse Commission
1942 Hamilton Street
Regina, SAS   S4P 3V7
(306) 787-4086
Library: (306) 787-4656

MANITOBA

Alcoholism Foundation of
  Manitoba
1031 Portage Avenue
Winnipeg, Manitoba
  R3G 0R8
(204) 944-6200
Library: (204) 944-6233

ONTARIO

Addiction Research
  Foundation
33 Russell Street
Toronto, Ontario   M5S 2S1
(416) 595-6000
Library: (416) 595-6144
Information Centre:
  (416) 595-6100

QUEBEC

Services de Programmes aux
   Personnes Toxicomanes
Ministere des Services
   Sociaux
1005 chemin Ste-foy,
   3e etage
Ville de Quebec, PQ
   G1S 4N4
(418) 643-9887

Le Centre Quebecois de
   Documentation en
   Toxicomanie (CQDT)
Domremy-Montreal
15 693, boul. Gouin Ouest
Sainte-Genevieve, PQ
   H9H 1C3
(514) 626-0220

NEW BRUNSWICK

Department of Health &
   Community Services
PO Box 5100
Fredericton, NB   E3B 5G8
(506) 453-2581
Library: (506) 453-3800

NOVA SCOTIA

Drug Dependency Services
Lord Nelson Building,
   6th floor
5675 Spring Garden Road
Halifax, NS   B3J 1H1
(902) 424-4270

PRINCE EDWARD ISLAND

PEI Addiction Services
Central Office
PO Box 37
Charlottetown, PEI   C1A 7K2
(902) 368-4028

NEWFOUNDLAND

Department of Health
Drug Dependency Services
1st floor, Conf. Bldg,
   West Block
PO Box 8700
St. John's, Newfoundland
   A1B 4J6
(709) 729-0623
fax (709) 729-5824

Library
8th floor, Southcott Hall,
Forest Road, PO Box 8700
(709) 729-0732
fax (709) 729-2165
Att: Heather Cooke

NORTHWEST TERRITORIES

Alcohol, Drugs & Community
   Mental Health Services
Department of Social Services
Box 1320
Yellowknife, NWT   X1A 2L9
(403) 873-7709

This book is published by the Alliance for a Drug-Free Canada, a charitable organization (#0804591-57) created by major business corporations in Canada to provide for education on the harm that can result from substance abuse.

Alliance Partners in 1993 include the following:

Air Canada
Bank of Nova Scotia
Bombardier Inc.
Bristol-Myers Squibb
   Pharmaceuticals
Canada Post Corporation
Canadian National
Cohn & Wolfe

CP Rail
Imperial Oil Limited
Kraft General Foods
Mediacom Inc.
Noranda Inc.
Oshawa Group Limited
Procter & Gamble Inc.

For more information on the Alliance for a Drug-Free Canada, please call toll-free 1-800-563-5000.

This book has been reviewed and approved by the Addiction Research Foundation.

The Addiction Research Foundation, founded in 1949, conducts specialized research, educational, clinical and community service development programs throughout the Province of Ontario. As well, the Foundation has been designated a collaborating centre for research and training on drug dependence by the World Health Organization.

ARF is a non-profit agency of the Province of Ontario.

For more information on the Foundation, its products or services, please contact us at:

Addiction Research Foundation
33 Russell Street
Toronto, Ontario
M5S 2S1

In Ontario, call toll-free
1 (800) INFO-ARF

In Toronto, or outside of Ontario:
(416) 595-6111